I am Sheriauna

Book 2

WE ARE ABLE

Written by: Sherylee Honeyghan

Illustrated by: Ana Patankar

Publication date July 2021
Printed by Kindle Direct Publisher

"For when I am weak, then I am strong"
II Corinthians 12: 10 NKJV

Sheriauna, your commitment to achieving your goals doesn't stop amazing me. Your ability to set your intention - believe, do the work, and hold the positive energy even when things get hard - and see your dreams manifest is beautiful to watch. Continue to lead others by your examples and remember that you are limitless.

Note to Parents/Guardians/Caregivers:

I hope that you and your child (ren) enjoy reading this book together. The first book in the I Am Sheriauna series was meant to be an introduction to Sheriauna. This second book shares some memorable experiences where Sheriauna had to overcome some challenges in order to achieve her goals. This book was created to share the triumphs but also to show young ones that it is alright if you don't get it the first time; with practice, perseverance, and persistence it will happen!

My hope is to create awareness in children from a young age about people with differences so that they can become more accepting of others. Diversity and inclusion are important in a world where we are all human but unique in our own ways. Hopefully this is a great resource to open up a dialogue with your children about people who have amputations or may be different from them, and answer their questions in a safe environment.

Note to Teachers:

You have such a large role in the lives of our children as you teach them and interact with them during a large part of their day. Please use this book to create an opportunity to discuss differences, curiosity and questions vs. jeering and staring. You may not have a child in the class who has an amputation but your students will come across a child or adult one day who may have a mild or severe disability or just look different from them and my hope is that one conversation, one book, may make a difference. This is also an opportunity to discuss topics like practicing and developing a skill, trying, hard work, setting goals, and overcoming adversity.

Some words are highlighted in BLUE. Please see the glossary at the back of this book for definitions as a tool to help explain some of the technical words to readers.

SUMMER TIME
I am so excited to see you again because I have something to tell you.
Guess what?
HI!
It's me. Sheriauna.

I learned how to
ride my BIKE!
JUST 2 WHEELS
Riding my bike!
Right hand... Left hand... Right hand... Left hand!
AND climb the monkey bars this Summer!

Ok so first I had a **tricycle** when I was younger...
SUMMER TIME
my first tricycle!
...and I would just lean over and use
my left arm to control the handle and balance.

It wasn't too hard because I had 3 wheels
but this summer my Mommy & Daddy bought me a bigger bike.
My new bike is pink
with white handles.
It has two big wheels with **small training wheels** at the back.

I could still use my left arm to balance on my new bike but it is not very good for my posture;
I end up leaning over too much.
The best thing for me to do was to get a new attachment to go on...
...my prosthetic limb also known as my helper arm.

BIKE ATTACHMENT
The socket part screws into my prosthetic arm
and the ball part is fitted onto the handle of my bike.
I always wear my helmet for safety.
...and once I hear it...
CLICK
I push my arm and socket down onto the ball...
...I am ready to go!

So I was riding almost every day with my training wheels until one day I decided to try riding without them.
I was really scared and thought...
What if I fall off? I mean how will I fall?
Will my arm get stuck?

Mommy and Daddy showed me how to pull my prosthetic arm out of the socket so that I could fall safely if I needed to.
That is a lot of stuff to think about ON TOP of actually riding your bike.
Phew!

Here we go!
I'm riding a 2 wheeler!!!
JUST 2 WHEELS
YAY!
I feel so happy and proud...
Oh no!! There's a bump in the sidewalk.
AAAHHHHHH!

It's ok Sheriauna. You're alright and you did it all by yourself!
I rode my bike by myself for the first time without training wheels!
I just kept practicing and I fell less and less. When I did fall I wasn't as scared.

One day I rode my bike to the park with Daddy and we tried the monkey bars.
Monkey bars
He normally helps me across but I told him that I wanted to try and cross the bars myself.
I want to try myself

To start
I stepped up on the platform
and took a big breath.
DEEP BREATH!
IT'S SUMMER
...HERE I GO!
Then I jumped up and grabbed
the bar with my right hand and
quickly swung my left arm up
to hold on really tight.

Then I swung to put my right arm on the next bar and-I FELL!
That happened many times over the next few days.
I would make it an extra bar then fall. Get back up, do it again and fall.
AARGGGHHHH!!!
My arms were so tired and I was getting really frustrated I started to cry and Daddy gave me a big hug and told me that we can try again tomorrow.

The next day,
we went back to the park
and I got ready to cross
those monkey bars.
SUMMER VIBES!
FUN
Hurray!

This helper arm is called a recreational or passive limb...
...and I loooooove it so much!!!!
Dance Dance Dance!!

This limb helps me do so many different activities because I can change the attachments on the end.
For example, my bike attachment is a ball and socket.
To play the guitar I use a pick attachment.

I sometimes use a fin attachment to swim.
To dance and do gymnastics, I use my favourite attachment... mushroom tumbler.
Summer!
I'll tell you more about that another day

Want to know what makes this day even better?
I am all packed...
...to go to England with my Nana today!
PASSPORT

Just remember to never give up on yourself.
We all have a different way of doing things sometimes.
...but if you believe in yourself and work at it, you can do it!
YOU CAN DO IT

I'm off now!
..but before I go, keep being kind to others..
Good bye
..and I'll see you next time!

GLOSSARY

Posture:
The position or bearing of the body whether characteristic or assumed for a special purpose

Prosthesis:
An artificial device to replace or augment a missing or impaired part of the body

Attachment:
A device attached to a machine or implement

Frustrated:
Feeling discouragement, anger, and annoyance because of unresolved problems or unfulfilled goals, desires, or needs

Source:

Merriam-Webster Incorporated (2020). Dictionary. https://www.merriam-webster.com/

Thanks & Gratitude

I truly believe that each person is here for a reason. We all have a purpose and I am so grateful that God has revealed mine to me through this journey. I continue to be thankful for my 3 greatest blessings; my children who are my greatest teachers. Sheriauna, Jeremiah and Samuel continue to teach me how to be more patient, more gracious, more understanding, more confident, and more grateful each and every day.

Jeffrey, thank you for always taking the time to create a safe space for Sheriauna to try new things. When she gets frustrated you give her room to take a break and return back to it when she is ready because the desire to accomplish the goal is still there. Thank you for always having your camera ready to capture these precious moments too!

To my family (Mom, Dad, Mark and Tonya) for always being supportive and being an integral part of my village, thank you. You are all our biggest cheerleaders and I know that no matter what you will continue to be there for me and my children.

Extended family and friends who are family, thank you for always supporting whether it was attending events, purchasing my first book, sharing the book with others, and positively speaking my name and lifting up my mission in rooms where I was not present, I am grateful for you and thank you.

Ana and Mukul, once again you have demonstrated your talents and abilities in this project. Thank you for taking the time to consult with me and now Sheriauna to ensure that this book is authentic to our story and the personal touches are engrained throughout each page.

I am grateful for each person that has read I Am Sheriauna: We are Beautiful and reached out to share their own stories or to share how Sheriauna's story impacted them and their children. I do not take any of it for granted and I want you to know that you are appreciated.

www.ingramcontent.com/pod-product-compliance
Ingram Content Group UK Ltd.
Pitfield, Milton Keynes, MK11 3LW, UK
UKHW060114300726
14090UKWH00002B/193

* 9 7 9 8 4 7 1 6 6 9 4 9 9 *